Library of Congress Control Number: 2002115220

ISBN 0-7624-1619-X

This book may be ordered by mail from the publisher. Please include $1.00 for postage and handling.
But try your bookstore first!

Running Press Book Publishers
125 South Twenty-second Street
Philadelphia, Pennsylvania 19103-4399

Log onto www.specialfavors.com to order Running Press® Miniature Editions™ with your own custom-made covers!

Visit us on the web!
www.runningpress.com

Introduction

Sometimes a single phrase can
alter the way we see the world
and forever change the way
we see ourselves. In this second
collection of *Quotable Women*,
the voices of famous females

from the past and the present
reveal the lessons they have
learned during their own personal odysseys. Proving once
again that common bonds
unite women through the ages,
inside you'll find the wit and
wisdom of women from many

nations, religions, walks of life,

and schools of thought.

In this book you'll also find

mothers, daughters, friends,

sisters, lovers, and dreamers

sharing their thoughts on

the ins and outs of life, from

the love that moves us, to the

heartaches that bring us to our knees. Above all, this collection is a testament to the strength and courage of those who have gone before us, and is sure to be an inspiration for all women on their journey through life.

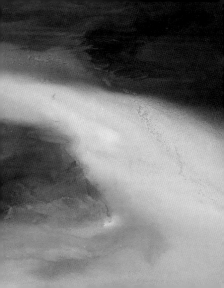

If high heels were
so wonderful,
men would still be
wearing them.

Sue Grafton
American author

Women complain about
premenstrual syndrome,
but I think of it as
the only time of the month
that I can be myself.

Roseanne Barr
American comedienne and actress

Old age is no place for sissies.

Bette Davis
(1908–1989)
American actress

It's not how
old you are,
but how
you are old.

Marie Dressler
(1869–1934)
American silent film actress

So much has been said
and sung of beautiful
young girls, why don't
somebody wake up to
the beauty of old women?

Harriet Beecher Stowe
(1811–1896)
American abolitionist author

I'm not offended by all the
dumb blonde jokes
because I know I'm
not dumb . . . . I also know
that I'm not blonde.

Dolly Parton
American singer

I am my own woman.

Maria Eva (Evita) Duarte de Peron
(1919–1952)
Argentine political leader

It is a curious thought,
but it is only when you see
people looking ridiculous
that you realize just
how much you love them.

Agatha Christie
(1890–1976)
British author

The ultimate lesson
all of us have to learn is
unconditional love,
which includes not only
others but ourselves as well.

**Elizabeth Kubler-Ross,
Swiss psychiatrist and author**

Do not think that love,
in order to be genuine,
has to be extraordinary.
What we need is to love
without getting tired.

Mother Teresa (Agnes Gonxha Bojaxhiu)
(1910–1997)
Albanian nun and humanitarian

Walking with a friend
in the dark
is better than walking
alone in the light.

Helen Keller
(1880–1968)
American author and educator

When love turns away,
now, I don't follow it.
I sit and suffer,
unprotesting, until I feel
the tread of another step.

Sylvia Ashton-Warner
(1908–1984)
New Zealander educator, author, and poet

Life ought to be a struggle of desire toward adventures whose nobility will fertilize the soul.

Rebecca West
(1892-1983)
Irish author and journalist

Perhaps the most delightful friendships are those in which there is much agree- ment, much disputation, and yet more personal liking.

George Eliot (aka Mary Ann Evans)
(1819–1880)
British novelist

Love is the only
shocking act
left on the face
of the earth.

Sandra Bernhard
American actress and comedienne

I leave you my portrait
so that you will
have my presence all the
days and nights
that I am away from you.

Frida Kahlo
(1907–1954)
Mexican painter

Never bend your
head. Hold it high.
Look the world
straight in the eye.

Helen Keller
(1880–1968)
American author and educator

Age does not protect
you from love.
But love, to some
extent, protects
you from age.

Jeanne Moreau
French actress

You cannot shake hands with a clenched fist.

Indira Gandhi
(1917–1984)
Indian politician

I think laughter may be a form of courage. . . . As humans we sometimes stand tall and look into the sun and laugh, and I think we are never more brave than when we do that.

Linda Ellerbee
American broadcast journalist

It is better to
be a lion for a day
than a sheep
all your life.

Sister Elizabeth Kenny
(1886–1952)
Australian nurse

I never intended
to become
a run-of-the-mill
person.

Barbara Jordan
(1936–1996)
American politician

You have to admit that most
women who have done
something with their
lives have been disliked
by almost everyone.

Françoise Gilot
French painter

Never doubt that a small group of thoughtful, committed citizens can change the world. Indeed, it is the only thing that ever has.

Margaret Mead
(1901–1978)
American anthropologist

Those who do not
know how to weep
with their whole
heart don't know
how to laugh either.

Golda Meir
(1898–1978)
Israeli Prime Minister

The best thing
that can come with
success is the
knowledge that it is
nothing to long for.

Liv Ullmann
Norwegian actress and humanitarian

I don't want to be
a passenger
in my own life.

Diane Ackerman
American poet and essayist

Independence is happiness.

Susan B. Anthony
(1820–1906)
American suffragist

There is nothing
stronger in
the world than
gentleness.

Han Suyin
Chinese author and physician

If we mean to have
heroes, statesmen,
and philosophers,
we should have
learned women.

Abigail Adams
(1744–1818)
American Former First Lady

Why get married and
make one man
miserable when I can
stay single and make
thousands miserable?

Carrie Snow
American comedienne

No book has yet been written
in praise of a woman who
let her husband and children
starve or suffer while she
invented even the most useful
things, or wrote books,
or expressed herself in art,
or evolved philosophic systems.

Anna Garlin Spencer
(1851–1931)
American feminist minister and writer

Educate a woman and you educate a family.

Jovita Idar
(1885–1946)
Mexican-American jounalist,
political activist, and teacher

She was the archetypal self-less mother: living only for her children, sheltering them from the consequences of their actions—and in the end doing them irreparable harm.

Marcia Muller
American author

I have yet to
hear a man ask for
advice on how to
combine marriage
and a career.

Gloria Steinem
American feminist author

When motherhood becomes
the fruit of a deep yearning,
not the result of ignorance
or accident, its children
will become the foundation
of a new race.

Margaret Sanger
(1879–1966)
American birth control advocate

I never married because there was no need. I have three pets at home which answer the same purpose as a husband. I have a dog which growls every morning, a parrot which swears all afternoon and a cat that comes home late at night.

Marie Corelli
(1855–1924)
British author

Feminism—I myself have never
known what feminism is.
I only know that people call me
a feminist whenever I express
sentiments that differentiate me
from a doormat or a prostitute.

**Rebecca West
(1892–1985)
British author and journalist**

If the world were
a logical place,
men would
ride sidesaddle.

Rita Mae Brown
American author and social activist

Would men but generously snap our chains, and be content with rational fellowship instead of slavish obedience, they would find us more observant daughters, more affectionate sisters, more faithful wives, more reasonable mothers—in a word, better citizens.

Mary Wollstonecraft
(1759–1797)
British feminist writer

The most exciting thing
about women's liberation
is that this century will
be able to take advantage
of talent and potential
genius that have been
wasted because of taboos.

Helen Reddy
American singer

To wear your heart
on your sleeve
isn't a very good plan;
you should wear it inside,
where it functions best.

Margaret Thatcher
British Prime Minister

Women dress alike
all over the world:
they dress
to be annoying to
other women.

Elsa Schiaparelli
(1890–1973)
Italian-French designer

A pedestal is
as much a prison
as any other
small space.

Gloria Steinem
American feminist author

I do not wish
women to have
power over men;
but over themselves.

Mary Wollstonecraft
(1759–1797)
British feminist writer

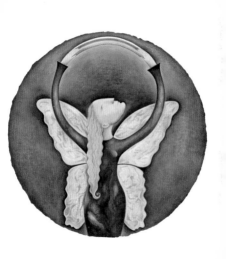

Lots of people want to ride
with you in the limo,
but what you want
is someone who will take
the bus with you
when the limo breaks down.

Oprah Winfrey
American television personality

Cowards falter,
but danger is often
overcome by those
who nobly dare.

Queen Elizabeth
(1900–2002)
British monarch

I am building a fire,
and everyday I train,
I add more fuel.
At just the right moment,
I light the match.

Mia Hamm
American professional soccer player

Nagging is the
repetition
of unpalatable
truths.

Baroness Edith Summerskill
(1901–1980)
British physician and politician

If you can't change
your fate,
change your attitude.

Amy Tan
Chinese-American author

Thank goodness I was
never sent to school;
it would have rubbed off
some of the originality.

Beatrix Potter
(1866–1943)
British author and illustrator

It is not enough
to reach for the brass ring.
You must also
enjoy the merry-go-round.

Julie Andrews
British singer, actress, and author

How wonderful it is that nobody need wait a single moment before starting to improve the world.

Anne Frank
(1929–1945)
Dutch author and Holocaust victim

Be on the alert to
recognize your
prime at whatever
time of your
life it may occur.

Muriel Spark
Scottish novelist and satirist

Nobody objects to a woman
being a good writer or sculptor
or geneticist if at the same time
she manages to be a good wife,
good mother, good looking,
good tempered, well groomed,
and unaggressive.

Leslie McIntyre
American feminist shamanic practitioner

I read and walked for miles at night along the beach, writing bad blank verse and searching endlessly for someone wonderful who would step out of the darkness and change my life. It never crossed my mind that that person could be me.

Anna Quindlen
American author and columnist

An aim in life is the only fortune worth finding.

Jacqueline Kennedy Onassis
(1929-1994)
American former First Lady and editor

One test of the
correctness of
educational procedure
is the happiness
of the child.

Maria Montessori
(1870–1952)
Italian educator

It's not true I had nothing on,
I had the radio on.

Marilyn Monroe
(1926–1962)
American actress

I have come finally to a
simple philosophy of work.
I enjoy what I do
and do the best I can.
That is enough.

Maria Schell
Austrian actress

The future belongs
to those who believe
in the beauty
of their dreams.

Eleanor Roosevelt
(1884–1962)
American former First Lady

There came a time when
the risk to remain
tight in the bud was more
painful than the
risk it took to blossom.

**Anais Nin
(1903–1977)
French author**

When people keep
telling you that you
can't do a thing, you
kind of like to try it.

Margaret Fuller
(1810–1850)
American author and lecturer

Distance doesn't matter; it's only the first step that is difficult.

Marie de Vichy-Chamrond
(1697–1780)
French Marquise

It's going to
be a long hard drag,
but we'll make it.

Janis Joplin
(1943–1970)
American singer

There are no
shortcuts
to any place
worth going.

Beverly Sills
American opera singer

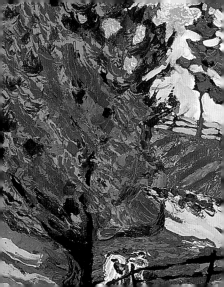

Truth isn't
always beauty,
but the
hunger for it is.

Nadine Gordimer
South African author and Nobel
Laureate in Literature

If you have not forgiven yourself something, how can you forgive others?

Dolores Huerta
American labor activist

I'd rather have
roses on my
table than diamonds
on my neck.

Emma Goldman
(1869–1940)
American anarchist

The one important thing
I have learned over the years is
the difference between
taking one's work seriously and
taking one's self seriously.
The first is imperative,
and the second is disastrous.

Margot Fonteyn
(1919–1991)
British ballet dancer

The trouble with most people is that they think with their hopes or fears or wishes rather than with their minds.

**Nancy Astor
(1879–1964)
British politician**

The main thing
in one's own
private world is
to try to laugh as
much as you cry.

Maya Angelou
American author and poet

Men travel faster now,

but I do not know

if they go to better things.

Willa Cather
(1873–1947)
American author

Things are going
to get a lot
worse before
they get worse.

Lily Tomlin
American comedienne and actress

A sobering thought:
what if,
at this very moment,
I am living up
to my full potential?

Jane Wagner
American writer and director

The truly fearless
think of them-
selves as normal.

Margaret Atwood
Canadian author

I began to have an idea
of my life, not as the slow
shaping of achievement
to fit my preconceived
purposes, but as the gradual
discovery and growth of a
purpose which I did not know.

Joanna Field
British psychologist

Art Credits

Front cover: *Sweet Life*, detail (1985), by Mahvash. Courtesy of the artist, www.mahvashmossaed.com.

Back cover and p. 87: *Spring* (2002), by Roxana Villa. Courtesy of the artist, www.RoxanaVilla.com.

p. 5: *Three Women* (1999), by Jane Mjolsness. Courtesy of the artist, www.janemjolsness.com.

pp. 8–9: *Cascade* (1993), by Diana Kan. © Diana Kan/Licensed by VAGA, New York, NY.

p. 14: *Retablo Para Mi Hermana Rosario Sánchez Cardenas* (1994), by Marta Sánchez. Courtesy of William and Kathy Kulik.

pp. 18–19: *Mahina* (1990), by Pegge Hopper. Courtesy of The Pegge Hopper Gallery, Honolulu, HI, www.peggehopper.com.

pp. 22–23: *Mi Familia* (ca. 1995), by Kelly Stribling Sutherland. Courtesy of the artist, www.friendandjohnson.com.

p. 26: *Black Girl with Wings* (1997), by Laura James. Private collection/Bridgeman Art Library.

pp. 30–31: *In the Garden* (1995), by Mahvash. Courtesy of the artist, www.mahvashmossaed.com.

p. 35: *Lorissa* (2002), by Rachel Bliss. Collection of Margaret Souders.

p. 39: *Irish Cottage*, detail (ca. 1935–38), by Josephine Joy. Smithsonian American Art Museum, Washington, DC/Art Resource, NY.

pp. 42–43: *Orange Vase, Orange Poppies* (1996), by Janet Fish. © Janet Fish/Licensed by VAGA, New York, NY.

p. 46: *Amoryllis*, detail (2003), by Roxana Villa. Courtesy of the artist, www.RoxanaVilla.com.

p. 50: *Bad Girl* (1998), by Shelley Spector. Photo by Elena Bouvier. Courtesy of Sande Webster Gallery, Philadelphia.

pp. 54–55: *Katmandu* (1999), by Sica. Courtesy of Sande Webster Gallery, Philadelphia.

p. 58: *Quiet Time* (2000), by Kelly Stribling Sutherland. Courtesy of the artist, www.friendandjohnson.com.

pp. 64–65: *Living in a Miniature Doll House* (1997), by Mahvash. Courtesy of the artist, www.mahvashmossaed.com.

p. 71: *Miss Lou 3* (1996), by Rachel Bliss. Private collection.

p. 75: *Mariposa* (2003), by Roxana Villa. Courtesy of the artist, www.RoxanaVilla.com.

p. 78: *Autumn Leaves Fluttering in the Breeze* (1973), by Alma Woodsey Thomas. Smithsonian American Art Museum, Washington, DC/Art Resource, NY.

pp. 82–83: *Country Scene* by Malcah Zeldis. Malcah Zeldis/Art Resource, NY.

p. 90: *A Woman Reading* (1997), by Laura James. Private collection/Bridgeman Art Library.

pp. 94–95: *The Swim, or Two Mothers and their Children*

on a Boat (1910), by Mary Cassatt. Réunion des Musées Nationaux/Art Resource, NY.

p. 98: *Mixed Messages #14* (2002), by Gwen Maleson. Courtesy of Rosenfeld Gallery, Philadelphia.

p. 102: *Carefree* (ca. 1996), by Kelly Stribling Sutherland. Courtesy of the artist, www.friendandjohnson.com.

pp. 106–107: *Mr. Scott's Springhouse* (1999), by Helen Mirkil. Courtesy of the artist.

p. 110: *Woman with Flowers* (2000), by Jane Mjolsness. Courtesy of the artist, www.janemjolsness.com.

p. 115: *Las Hermanas Woloff* (1997), by Marta Sánchez. Courtesy of the artist, www.artedemarta.com.

p. 119: *Self-portrait* (1994), by Rachel Bliss. Courtesy of Snyderman Gallery, Philadelphia.

pp. 122–123: *Postcard from the Forest* (2002), by Doris Nogueira-Rogers. Courtesy of Sande Webster Gallery, Philadelphia.